Manhood

By Sundiata L. Sims

Empowerment Publishing & Multi-Media

Sundiata L. Sims

Sundiata L. Sims

ISBN: 13: 9781098861490

DEDICATION

I dedicate this book to my father, Samuel Lee Sims, my Superman. Thank you, Daddy. Also, to Sundiata L. Sims Jr. the two years God allowed me to be your father, I am grateful.

CONTENTS

ACKNOWLEDGMENTS

To my best friend, 'Shero' and daily inspiration, Carmalita A Longino-Sims, thank you for your encouragement and support.

To my children (Mikayla, Suniece and Sundi Jr.) whatever I do it's for you all to have a better tomorrow.

To my grandfather, Charley H Lowery, thank you for your inspiration and the life you lived.

To my uncles, James Lowery, Ed Lowery, Charles "Junior" Lowery, Joe Lowery, Grant Lowery, Ralph Mattox, Melvin Mattox and Willie "Shawn" Mattox, thank you.

To my cousins, all of them and there are a lot, thanks for your love and prayers.

To my Football coaches from Pee Wee ball to College, thank you.

To my mom J. Carol Lowery Sims, for always encouraging me to be the best I can be and for always reminding me, I can do all things through Christ who strengthens me.

To my 'ride or dies' my sisters, Kelly Lynn and Shawnna LaMonda (lol) thank you.

To Lisa Santiago McNeill and Brian K. McNeill, I can't thank The Empowerment Duo enough.

To Overseer Terry M Clark, your leadership and encouragement is immeasurable. To Micah-Aiden, the grandboy,   this   is   for   you!

1 TRAINING CHILDHOOD
The first step to Manhood starts during your childhood.

The experiences of childhood greatly affect your walk as a man. Many boys do not have the advantage of seeing the actions and behavior of men in their daily lives. It is in those early years a boy learns how he will communicate and the behaviors that will follow him throughout his lifetime. As I walk through my adult life, I reflect greatly on all the lessons I learned during my childhood. Today as when I was a child, I learned respect and manners can get you further than even knowledge and skills. As a 43-year-old I still address people as Mr. or Mrs. As I reflect on my early years, daily I can gain an even greater respect for all the things my parents and the other adults in my life taught me. The foundation, of the early years of my life, still benefits me every day as an adult. Over the years the values my parents instilled such as honesty, hard work and taking responsibility has help me maneuver through the obstacles of my life and I have gained and even greater appreciation for every lesson I was taught.

As I reflect back, I am very thankful that all my life I was encouraged that I could do anything that I put my mind to. I find it disheartening when I see on television and movies someone tell a young child that they are worthless, or they will not be anything. As a boy and even today, I still carry the belief that I can do whatever my mind is set to do. I would encourage every parent not to stifle their son or daughter by giving them mental limits. I truly believe every individual has the ability to do whatever they put their mind to do.

While growing up, I remember many saying they wanted to be the first Black President. I am thankful in my life I was able to see it as reality. The world we live in today truly has no limits to what a person can do. We as adults have to keep in mind, we hold a major key in shaping young men's life. The early year should be a time of exploration and growth. I think all parents should take their children to museums, art galleries and aquariums, so they don't have to limit themselves to just what they see in their neighborhood. Remember someone had to believe they could fly to the moon before ever attempting such a feat.

Having men in a boy's life

As an adult I value greatly the fact that I had a father, a grandfather, uncles and older male cousin in my life. My father who took an active role in every aspect of my life. I find this even more fascinating because of the fact my father grew up without his father. The most prominent lessons that the men in my life taught me, are not ones that I was sat down, and we talked through but were actions I was able to experience and see.

My father and mother both got up and worked, daily. They showed up on time and gave a full day's work. My parents taught me, and my sister's no honest work is shameful, but is a thing of honor and should be respected. My father gave of himself not just to me his son, but to numerous young men. My father was a man that would give life lesson to any young man he came across. My image of myself and my willingness and ability to stand on my own I credit to my father. The path to having a man with standards is seeing that example in childhood. The Bible's Proverb 22:6 says, "Train up a child in the way he should go, and when he is old, he will not depart from it." This Proverb is so true in my life and in any boy's life.

A boy needs to constantly see examples of manhood in his formative years. I was lucky, not only did I have my father as a guide, but I had uncles, my maternal grandfather, my father's friends, cousins, neighbors and coaches, that passed on their knowledge and guidance to me. I can say I have been truly blessed with the richness of male mentors I have been blessed to have in my life.

"When you are a boy" lessons

As a boy, one of the greatest blessings was the ability to be involved in sports and other activities that allowed interaction with other men and boys. Things like Boy's Scout and Pee Wee football were great place for me to learn lesson of manhood. Simple and practical things can be done to teach boys discipline, honor and respect. I give a lot of credit to my father for the man I am today, but there were also other men who, I can credit with influencing me as well. My first football coach Paul, showed me how to play a game that I would love for a lifetime. Coach Ed Mignery, my high school football coach. Jim Ladd, my high school coach and lineman coach. Coach

Ladd, I swore up and down that man hated me, but as I have grown and matured, I believe he gave me some of the most needed lessons of life.

Coach Ladd always made sure I worked hard and would not let me slack off or get a big ego. He also taught me how to really work for what I wanted. I swear I would work harder just to show him up, I did not believe he wanted me there, but he made me a good and discipline player. I will never forget my 11th grade year when he made me play a Junior Varsity game, after I only played 3 quarters the night before in the varsity game. I was so mad; I had never played in a JV game not even in my 10th grade year. I believed he had it out for me and 3rd quarter it would come to a head. After a series of offensive plays, he called me to the side line, I said, "Bet" and started running off the field. When I got to the sideline, he started ripping me a new one and I could not take it. I flew into a rage and cussed him out and threw off my shoulder pads, I was ready to quit the team and football. After my blow up I remembered my father was in the stands, I just knew that he was going to get me for my behavior. Surprisingly my father came to me and just said, "Put your shoulder pads on so you don't catch a cold." A few minutes later Coach Ladd asked me had I calm down and put me back in the game. My dad or my coach never said another word about the blow up I had. Coach Ladd never let me be just good on that field and in retrospect, during the JV game I was going thru the motions because I did not want to be there, but the encounter made me mad enough to play at my best.

Another man that I looked at as a mentor and have great respect for is Willie Walker; he was the President of the Dayton Urban League. Watching how Mr. Walker schmooze with powerful people and people seemed to really just like him. He was the total package as a businessman and social leader. He could get things done, and it all seems to be easy for him.

As the years have gone by, I have gained even more respect for the man he is. When you meet an outstanding person you just know it.

The first 11 years of my life I had the experience and the pleasure to get to know, Charlie Hubbard Lowery, my maternal grandfather. Today, as a grown man, I still want to be like him. He was born in the late 1890's in Alabama, his mother was Irish, and his father was black. He raised 16 kids and had a knack for making all of his grandkids, all 50 or 60 of them feel like they were the special one. To this day, I still know I was his favorite.

That would have been enough, but he did more, he moved his family from the deep south, to Ohio, where he would start a junk yard and by the time he sold it, rumor has it that it was worth over a million dollars, in 1980's money. He was a real-life hero to me; I will never forget how he stopped a runaway mule, which yours truly was on playing cowboy. He was a much-disciplined man, who everyone seems to respect. I never heard anyone, beside my grandmother; refer to him without saying Mr. or Deacon. He has been dead for many years, but still when his children speak of him, they still get emotional.

The experience of manhood never stops and came to me in many different ways. As a pre-teen who enjoyed life, one day my dad told me to come with him; He took me to a local golf course and told me I was going to be a caddy, I said, "A what?" He said, "A caddy," and told me it was a great way to make some extra money. I was all in at first. At this point I need to let everyone know I probably was the worst caddy that had ever been. Who knew, I would have to study and pass a test to be a caddy.

Well, I passed, and a class B caddy I was. I will never forget one guy whose bag I carried; he would put his golf ball in his mouth as he went from one hole to the next tee, gross. I would always volunteer to go to the high ground to spot the balls. I volunteered for two reasons. One, another caddy had to carry my bag and two, I had no clue where the ball went, but I could chill for a minute. I will admit I had no clue where the balls landed, half the time I wouldn't even be looking. I did enjoy being a caddy. While caddying, I would hear the players talk about business, their families or their game. I learned real deals happen on the golf course. Caddying taught me about work ethic and responsibility. Funny even the world's worst caddy can learn from the experience.

A couple of years later, I got, at the time, what I thought was a teen's dream job. While working out at the Y, I found out about a job working at the local pool. I thought this would be fun. The job consisted of checking passes and collecting money at the front gate. I applied for the job and I got it. But before the season started, I had to go through a CPR and life safety class. I remember the life guards were all recent high school grads and college students. That summer they just keep playing John Cougar Mellencamp. 'Pink Houses for You and Me' and 'Jack and Diane' at nauseum. I would get in trouble for having kids around that I would be talking to.

But beside Mellencamp, all seem to be going well. One morning when I was opening, the assistant manager stop me and told me my till was short the day before. I was very confused. I had counted the till before I left. Not only had I counted it, but I did what my sister had told me to do when handling money especially someone else's money, I counted it three times. In retrospect I should have thought something was fishy, especially when he said we could not record a couple of the people that entered to make up the loss. At the time I thought he was cool. He must really like me to help me out. The truth would be revealed a couple of weeks later. When I was called in the manager's office and fired. I was stunned and I refused to sign a paper that said I had done something I had not.

I learned never acknowledge a lie about you or anyone else.

Years later, I found out that 'cool assistant' was the real culprit. He was taking the money. That experience taught me two very important things. One if you did not do anything wrong never allow someone to try and make you believe you did. Two, when someone sends you a life saver make sure it's not full of lead.

Now I am thankful for both life experience, I

took lesson from both jobs that I have used in both my personal and professional life.

CHAPTER 2: TIME TO GROW UP...

The summer of 1990 would be a life changing summer for me. I had completed my first year of college and I was home for the summer working. The day was like any other day, I worked at my former high school during the summer, nothing glamorous in any way, I was a summer janitor. So, I got up at 5:45 a.m. that morning, made it to work by 6:30 a.m., and did my summer janitorial duties. I got off by 3:30 p.m. and like always headed home. When I got home, I unlocked the door and went in the house, and I noticed no one was home. No one being home was not unusual but generally, in the summer, my mom would be home because she was a teacher and off during the summer. As I usually did, I went in the kitchen to get something to eat and drink. As I walked in the kitchen, I saw we had messages on our answering machine. Not thinking anything of it I pressed the play button like always and I heard it. It was my mom's voice, and she said, "Sundi, this is your mother, I'm with your father at Good Samaritan hospital, they are not sure if he has a collapsed lung or what, but they are doing test…"

I don't remember the rest I just went into panic mode; I didn't know what to do. This had never happened to me; I had never really had to deal with a real-life problem. I called my then girlfriend, Cheryl; she was a calming voice for me at that time. She calmed me down and instructed me to come and pick her up and we would go see what was going on. By the time I picked her up and we arrived at the hospital, I was a nervous wreck. You have to realize, how I saw my father. I saw my father as a Superman. He was the biggest, bravest person I knew, and nothing could harm him. So, to hear something was wrong with him, my mind could not comprehend.

I could not imagine it and to top that with the fear of hospitals and sick people did not help my situation. You have to realize at this point, the only relationship I had with someone truly being sick and having to be hospitalized, were relatives. A good deal of them had cancer and would very soon die. The mind can be a very different place when you let it run wild.

Seeing my father lying there and with all those tubes and who knows what all that junk was, I just could not take it. My father would have to be hospitalized for 31 days; he had pneumonia that had been there for quite a while and he end up having a third of his lung removed. It was a very traumatic time for my whole family. It was very hard for me. At first, I would not visit him in the hospital. After about a week of him being in the hospital I had not visited him, and my mom must of knew I was scared to visit him. One evening as we were talking about my father and his health, my mom said, "Why haven't you gone and visit your father." I gave no excuse, but told her, I did not want to see him in the hospital; the truth was I was scared to death to go. She scolded me and told me that I needed to go see my father, she expressed that he needed to see his children.

After that talk I did go and see him, but I did not go during the day, I would go in the middle of the night or very early in the morning. While he was still in the hospital, I had to take on more responsibility around our home. I remember feeling that it was my responsibility to take care of the house duties my father would do. As the days came and went my father was healing physically well. The time my father spent in the hospital greatly affected him mentally. I think he had time to reflect on his life and some of the shortcomings. Soon he would be coming home, and many changes would come. During his stay he realized he would have to stop smoking, so before my father got out of the hospital, he had me look throughout the house and remove the cigarette packs he had stashed throughout the house, and man did he have them everywhere. By the time it was all said and done I had gathered about 2 cartoons worth of cigarettes. My dad had smoked my entire life until that time. I still remember how I and my sisters would be sitting in the back of the car thinking surely, we are going to die from the smoke when we would take trips. Although, it has been over 20 years since he stopped smoking, I can still remember his brand, Viceroy Longs.

While in the hospital my dad had to confront a lot of demons that he had not dealt with but had haunted him his whole life and somewhat still do. My dad was his mother's only child and during the 40's and 50's to be a black male raised in a single parent home must have been a very difficult situation. My dad met his father when he was 13. I was not there but I can only imagine the meeting not being a good one. It seemed like for the rest of my dad's life, he wanted to get confirmation from his dad.

The man that my dad was told was his father was M.C. Mattox. I must say I never really cared for M.C. He was never very nice to me or my father. When I would be around him it was clear he was a good grandfather to his grandchildren… well all but me and my two sisters. I will never forget a time when we stop by to visit, several of his grandkids were there. I remember him taking all of the other kids to get ice cream, but made it clear me and my sisters were not invited to come. I never felt comfortable calling him granddad. My dad would always speak of him in terms of your grandfather, and I would have to catch myself from saying, "You mean M.C. Mattox." I never could understand why my dad wanted a relationship with him and why he took the disrespect he did, just to be around him. But as time has gone on, I understand every man wants to be accepted and validated by their father. Although M.C. is no longer here, in so many ways my father still looks to get his approval.

When my dad got home, he had changed in so many ways. He would do some irrational things. He became paranoid, and for a while he started drinking and to be honest before that time, I don't believe I had ever seen him drink any alcohol. I will never forget the first day he got out the hospital; he insisted that we (me and my mother) take him to an event sponsored by the School Board that he was the president of. I remember me and my mother begging him not to go, but he insisted. He could not even walk on his own and he was very weak, but he went. I remember the other board members faces when he walked in. They all looked stunned and immediately asked him why he had come in his weakened state.

I remember feeling embarrassed and I didn't want others to see my father in his weakened state. In retrospect, I believe that him going to the event on the day he was released from the hospital was his undoing on the school board. My father became very paranoid and mean after his hospital stay. He would carry his .38 with him everywhere he went. He also would lock every door, no matter if you had just step out and would be returning shortly. I soon realized that if I left without my keys, I wouldn't get back in.

I still do not know the full scope of what my father deals with, I do know that time alone, a time of just reflecting shocks him to his core. Later, my mother had me bury that gun out in the garden. Since I was the only one home, I caught the wrath of his misplaced anger. So, for a 2- or 3-year period I just tried to stay out of his way. When I look back on that time, I realize the anger came out of the pain he felt about things in his life. It was as if my father did not feel validated by his father or by society in general. It's crazy to me, because my father always encouraged me and I never felt like less than in any part of my life, but yet he felt that way about himself.

During that time, my father made some bad decisions. He made a bad investment; he committed adultery and even started drinking. All he did was in order not to face some of his own demons. Some people would have stayed there and never worked out of the rut, but true to the man I now him to be, he got some help and he was able to pull himself up and out of his funk and continued with life.

It makes me proud as a son, that my father could get down and make mistakes but be man enough to not allow his mistake to be an ending of a great guy, but a stumbling block he was able to get up from. My dad, for all his misgivings, he still amazes me with how good a heart he has. I have seen him by a meal for the homeless and get a suit for a kid to go to a school dance. I will never forget one day in particular. We were riding down the street and passed an older lady on the side of the road who had a flat tire. I thought nothing of it until my dad turned the car around and went back to where the lady was. He stops the car and got out to see if she needed help. The lady seemed very nervous, I guess I would be as well if I were an older white woman and two black males, I did not know approach me on the side of a road. Nervously she informed him she had a flat tire. I might add this was before the wide spread of cell phones. He went to ask if she had a spare. She indicated she did. My father instructed me to get out the car and we, or I should say 'I' proceeded to change the tire. My dad talked to her to put her at ease, and I changed the tire. As I was finishing up and closed her trunk, she went in her pocket and pulled out some money and offers it to us. Me in my teenage mind thought, "Bet, money." However, my dad just said, "Ma'am, no thank you, just put it in the offering plate." I remember as we drove off, I sat and was thinking, "Dad that was money, how could you refuse it?" My face must have revealed what I was thinking, because my father said to me, "Sometimes you do good just because."

CHAPTER 3: SOFTER SIDE

...for Adam there was not found a help meet for him. And the LORD God caused

a deep sleep to fall upon Adam, and he slept: and he took one of his ribs, and closed

up the flesh instead thereof; And the rib, which the LORD God had taken from man,

made he a woman and brought her unto the man. Genesis 2:20-22

I need to say this; *There is a difference between being a gentleman and a man.* But saying that, I believe you cannot talk about men without talking about the relationship to woman. My first love was and still is my mother. The older I get the more I can appreciate the balance of having both my father and mother in my life. There are times now and in my younger years I can appreciated and needed that feminine touch that my mother brings. It seems I mark my life by events and the 'woman', or in some cases 'women' that were in my life. From the age of birth to about 16, my mom and my sister were the women who played a great role in my life. They comforted me and supported me. I love those three without question.

My oldest sister, Kelly, I have always seen as fearless. Beside my father, Kelly was me and my sister Shawnna's protector. Kelly has always been serious in nature. She would have been an excellent soldier; she has always been a very organized and disciplined person. To this very day Kelly is the example of the oldest sibling that anyone could follow. For all her bossy ways, Kelly is very loving and caring, however she will tell you like it is, holding back no punches and back in the day would throw a couple of punches to get you to act right. My middle sister and I always knew if mom and dad were not around Kelly was the law.

My other sister Shawnna suffers from middle child syndrome, that's if you listen to her. She is very bright and so funny. It does not matter how down I get, within a minute of talking to Shawnna, I will be laughing, about only God knows what. Shawnna has always been 2 years in front of me in school, she would give me the lowdown about teachers and even helped to guide my way through high school and later college. Shawnna is my ride or die, her personality is more like my own. We both love to laugh and talk. Both Kelly and Shawnna are very smart and still to this day, they will drop all to come and make sure their younger brother is ok.

My mother is a teacher in profession and in every other moment of her life. J. Carol "Lowery" Sims is a very intelligent, reasonable and loving small-town girl. I love my mother dearly and I can always count on her. It's hard to describe my mother for me, I'm not sure why, maybe because of all she means to me, I can directly attribute my love of learning to my mom. Being one of 16 kids, family was very important to my mom. It's funny having that many aunts and uncles means I have more first cousins then most people have 'cousins' period. My mom is the one that built the belief in me that I could, truly, do anything I put my mind too. I remember when I struggled with spelling, like the teacher mom she is, she would have me read, and sometimes still does, the local newspaper. It helped me be a better reader and improve on my vocabulary. It gave me skills to do better on spelling test, but my spelling still sucks. I have always seen my mom as a strong woman, but her strength never was used to belittle my father. The way my mother would honor my father, she has and always will be a model wife to me. When she needs to 'take action,' she would, but she would always give my father room to act and if need be, she would put the groundwork down so that things would go smoothly for my dad.

From my parents I learned how a marriage partnership should work. Truly my dad weaknesses are my mom strength and the same in reverse. I have always taken pride in knowing that my mom could do most things on her own but chose to be in a partnership and when needed would take a back seat or the lead, whatever the situation called for.

Several other women have had a great impact on my life, my Grandmothers; Josephine Sims and Bessie Lee Lowery. My grandmothers where very different women, but they both showed love like only a grandmother could. My grandma Josephine would come to our house every Christmas. When we would stay at her house, she would let me and my sister's drink coffee. My grandma Josephine also had a very rich alto-tenor voice. It's hard to believe some of the wild stories I have heard about my grandma, from riding on the back of motorcycles to being the life of the party in her younger days.

My grandma Bessie actually took care of me for the first two weeks of my life. I was my mother's biggest baby and I ripped her pretty good, so she had to stay in the hospital for a week after my birth and the next week she came home to heal. My grandma Bessie always seem very regal to me. To this day no one can make biscuits or cookies like she could.

My mother's sisters, especially my aunt Jeanette and my aunt Ruth. My Aunt Ruth was my grandmother's oldest daughter. Aunt Ruth was much like Kelly in her role as an older sibling, if Aunt Ruth said it, it was done.

My Aunt Ruth was very sweet, but I remember watching her die of cancer, was truly heartbreaking.

My Aunt Jeanette is my mother's 'Shawnna.' Aunt Jeanette could make you laugh and without a doubt I know I was her favorite nephew. Aunt Jeanette and my mom were a year apart in age, and they were very close. My Aunt Jeanette was truly a second mom to me. She now and forever will be the only one that could get away with calling me 'Bumbee,' her nickname for me.

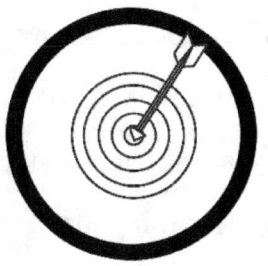

CHAPTER 4: SETTING GOALS

Through any man's life he needs to set goals and work to achieve them. Setting goals helps any man in developing self-discipline. Throughout my life I have had to consistently set new goals. Some goals need to be short-term and others over time. As a teenager I loved playing football. I would go to camps and absorb all I could about the sport I love.

I can remember my 8th grade year, the high school coach at the time spoke at our awards banquet. He gave a pretty standard banquet speech, but one thing he said stood out in my mind. He talked about the importance of the weight room. I knew that day I wanted to be the best I could be at playing football, and that I would become very familiar with the weight room. I had 2 goals I wanted to meet.

First, I wanted to be physically ready to play at the varsity level and two I wanted to be in the 250lb bench press club. I remember feeling a little nervous and scared, but I took a leap of faith and went to the high school weight room to work out. As I walked in, I know I looked like the scared and bewildered kid that I was. I was so relieved when a group of ninth grader I knew said, "Come on you can work out with us." I have to say I am very thankful for Sam Dunson, Matt Brown and Jeff Phipps, they let me join them and taught me how to work out. I can appreciate that they were just as faithful and dedicated to working out as I was. We would work out three days a week at school and I would leave the high school and go to the YMCA and continue to work out. I grew strong quickly and in a very short time I was able to do the weight and reps they were doing.

I had a goal of joining the 250 club; being able to lift 250lbs. I met it in my freshman year in High School. Next it would be playing at the varsity level. My next goal of being able to play at the varsity level was always on my mind. During my freshman year of High School, after our freshman season was over, all my extra time I would spend training. I would continue my weight room regimen as well as running a couple of times a week. When summer came, I stepped it up even more, summer workouts with the team. Then summer came to an end.

We had a new coach, Ed Mignery. Coach Mignery brought a new spirit to the team. From day one he made us believe we could be champions. I remember every practice I went all out. I made sure I took as many reps as I could. Coach Jim Ladd was our line coach and he made sure he pushed us. The first 3 games I played on every special team I could get on. Every time I hit the field I would go all out. The third game of the year the right offensive tackle Big Cline went down with a knee injury. On the following Monday after the game Coach Mignery called me and a junior, John "Plug" Harris, in his office. He said, "It's between you two who will fill Clines spot." At that moment I made up my mind that the spot was mine. You would have thought I was getting ready for a Superbowl that week!

I would do reps with the offense and when Plug was doing his reps, I would get reps playing defense. It got to a point that Coach Ladd would have to make me stop taking reps to give other people some reps. Well, Thursday came, and we are about to have our pre-game practice, and Coach Mignery says, "Alright Sundi, you got the spot, now see if you can keep it!" I never looked back, I was an offensive starter for the rest of that year and for the following 2 years.

The lesson and the blessing was not that I was a starter, but I learned a work ethic like no other. Even if I had never started, the work was worth it. I carried that tenacity to all things. I refuse not to give me best.

I wish I could sit here and pretend every goal I have set I have gotten. Well, I would be lying. Being human, we all can fall flat on our faces. But the lessons I learned playing football stand true; when you get knocked down don't just sit there, get up and keep moving forward.

CHAPTER 5 AN END AND A BEGINNING

My adventure from boyhood to manhood has been quite a journey. Along the way, I have had help by many men including my father, my grandfather, uncles, cousins, neighbors, teachers, coaches and mentors. I think the most insightful thing I can say is that manhood is a journey.

You don't just wake up one day and decide you are a man. There are a lot of steps involved. I think the most important step any boy can take is finding someone to pattern himself after. It's hard to do or be something you have never seen. No matter what someone tells you or says, in order to achieve manhood, you have to pattern yourself after a man. So, finding someone that you can pattern yourself after is the first choice a boy can make in his pursuit to manhood.

I am writing this book for the number of young men who have not had the advantage of having men in their lives. I am thankful for all the women who had to take on the task of raising boys. However as much as she may try, a woman, simply, cannot teach a boy to be a man. Teaching a boy to be polite and to open a door for a lady is nice, but that's not it. Being a man is about taking responsibility, being able to stand on your own two feet and deal with what comes your way. Standing and being able to take life is not easy. It's not to say woman cannot 'help' in the pursuit of manhood. A woman can help the young man be accountable for his actions and to guide him in decision making.

However, young man, you cannot sit down or lay around and let the world dictate who and what you are. I know as a man, I have had to make some tough decisions, I have also had to put myself second on many occasions. I had to sacrifice for the good of my family. I did these things without begrudging or belittling anyone. Manhood is not an easy pursuit. You don't come out of the womb being a man, there is a lot of learning involved.

The greatest men I know are men willing to listen to wisdom and learn from not only their own, but others mistake as well. It doesn't make you a man to be a 'bully' or try to 'boss' people around. It doesn't make you a man because you want to beat up everybody. Sometimes the best thing you can do as a man is to humble yourself.

For every young man that picks up this book to read, here are some things that I think will help on your journey:

1. Find a job - A man needs to have money in his pocket so you can do for yourself
2. Take responsibility - A man stands up to his responsibilities
3. Stand - It not easy to stand against the world but when you know something is right don't be shaken stand for what you believe in.

Remember there will be times when you feel lonely and even scared, there is nothing wrong with feeling lonely and scared, that just makes you human. What will define you as a man is how you deal with those emotions of fear and loneliness.

As a man of God, I know I am never truly alone. I have a lot of faith in you, young man. I and many more are praying for your success. We need more men; the world is counting on you.

ABOUT THE AUTHOR

Sundiata L. Sims is a caring, kind and loving husband and father. He is committed to God, his church, community and most of all his family. Sundiata serves as an amazing example of 'Manhood' for his children and grandson with his responsibility to provide, protect and direct them in life.

Sundiata is an integral part of M.E.N. (Male Empowerment Networks), a bi-monthly discussion group for men and teen-aged men ages 12+. By sharing his wisdom, listening and building relationships with men and teen-aged men, he is able to influence their lives in a positive way. Sundiata volunteers in the community and is very active in the church. He believes that by creating awareness, bringing insight and nurturing open dialog around the conversation of 'Manhood' he will be able to be a bridge for those who do not have a strong male mentor or father figure in their lives and help them to be better served to become the fathers, uncles, and grandfathers of tomorrow.

Sundiata L. Sims is a member of Body of Christ Assembly, in Charlotte, NC under the pastorship of Overseer Terry M. Clark. He resides in Charlotte, NC with his beautiful wife, Carmalita Longino Sims, their two daughters, Suniece and Mikayla and grandson Micah-Aiden, along with a host of family pets.

To book Sundiata to speak or conduct a workshop for your group, email: info@SundiataLSims.com